Finding Harmony with Horses
By
Connecting to
The Spirit
Within

Kylie Maree Dearden

BALBOA.
PRESS

A DIVISION OF HAY HOUSE

Balboa Press books may be ordered through booksellers or by contacting:

Balboa Press
A Division of Hay House
1663 Liberty Drive
Bloomington, IN 47403
www.balboapress.com.au
1-(877) 407-4847

Because of the dynamic nature of the Internet, any web addresses or
links contained in this book may have changed since publication and
may no longer be valid. The views expressed in this work are solely those
of the author and do not necessarily reflect the views of the publisher,
and the publisher hereby disclaims any responsibility for them.

Printed in the United States of America

ISBN: 978-1-4525-0214-4 (sc)
ISBN: 978-1-4525-0215-1 (e)

Any people depicted in stock imagery provided by Thinkstock are
models, and such images are being used for illustrative purposes only.
Certain stock imagery © Thinkstock.

Balboa Press rev. date: 10/17/2011

About the Author

Kylie Maree Dearden is a qualified Reiki 2 practitioner in natural healing. She has been attending spiritual development, meditation, physic and yoga classes for many years now. Kylie has completed a Certificate II in Equine Industry with the National Centre for Equine Education and is also a qualified horse coach and instructor with The Equestrian Federation of Australia. Kylie is the owner and founder of Finding Harmony with Horses, a horse instructing business that works on helping horse and rider become one in harmony. Kylie has experienced many rewarding moments with horses and owners during the 16 years she has been training and riding horses. Kylie was born at the Footscray hospital in Melbourne, Victoria, Australia on the 29th of June 1971.

Acknowledgments

I dedicate this book to my beloved horse Jess for being the guiding light to my soul. To all the other horses in the world, may they be loved and respected the way God intended them to be and may we learn to love and respect ourselves the way God intended.

I also dedicate this book to Louise L Hay and Dr Wayne W Dyer for their continued faith in me. They both have inspired me through their books over the years to be and give the best of myself that was possible. I am proud to say they have both played a big part in the loving person I am today.

I would like to thank my parents for bringing me into the world and caring for me and for their ongoing support and encouragement, also other family members and friends. My soul mate and dearest partner Lou for always been there for me, encouraging and helping me to grow into the best person I can be. I'd also like to thank my wonderful dog 'Monty' for his companionship, love and support. Last but not least The Universal Intelligence – God the white light for channelling through me this inspirational information which you are about to read by connecting to the spirit within.

*This book is dedicated to
all of the horse lovers of the world
Let's heal the world and make it a
better place for ourselves and our horses*

Introduction

We are now living in exciting times. We are evolving more and more each day. We are learning that through our relationships we grow and we are offered a chance to heal. If we are loved and nurtured, we are happy and fulfilled. Horses are naturally gifted to be able to love us unconditionally. God gave them this wonderful gift and yet we find it hard to find the same gift within ourselves. We hold onto our past pain and take that pain out on others. We are not aware of the effect this has on ourselves and our horses. We have much to learn from horses. If we remain open to their communication and take the time to observe and respect them, we will find harmony with them. They are always communicating to us messages, by listening and observing these messages and by using a positive approach; we will gain the horse's trust and respect.

I believe God joined me together with my beautiful horse to be healed.

God knew she had all the love I needed to make me into the loving person I am today. This I am eternally grateful to God for and grateful to my beautiful horse Jess, a bay Warmblood mare aged 16-years-old now. It has been 13 years of a spiritual journey with her that I will treasure for a lifetime.

I hope you enjoy reading my experiences I have had with my horse and horses in general. I hope I inspire you to go to your horse and open your heart and soul to it. It's waiting to love you and heal you.

It's waiting to embrace the light of your soul with its soul, so you can become one in harmony the way God intended it to be. Your horse is on your side, it wants you to see your inner beauty as it sees its own and yours.

Your horse will help you find it, if you let them. Your horse knows that this is its job; God has created your horse with all the tools to complete this task.

It's not about winning that competition or perfecting that movement. It's about honouring these magnificent spiritual beings of life and our own. We are never to take advantage of their kindness.

We are taking a quantum leap forward regarding the handling of horses now days. We are learning a healthier approach for the horse. We are letting go of the need to misuse our power and handle the horse in a threatening, harmful manner. We are learning to embrace our inner goodness and coming from love, understanding and compassion towards our horses. We are choosing to heal them, not hurt them, to love them not harm them. Your horse is waiting for you to give them a big hug and tell them how much you love them. By doing so you are pleasing God, the spirit within that loves you and once you find it within, it will guide you every step of the way to finding harmony with your horse. Never doubt it, it created you to express and embrace all of your divinity. It supports you, it has faith in you and so do I.

My beautiful Jess
You are the wind beneath my wings
I thank you for loving me
For having faith in me
For being patient with me
As we ride together we become one
In peace and harmony
With our creator God
We are ever so grateful
For this gift
Yours forever more
Kylie
by
Kylie Maree Dearden

Contents

Chapter 1:

A Spiritual journey, How I Found My Beautiful Horse

I connected to my soul's love again, thanks to my beautiful horse Jess. I always knew as I was growing up I had something special to share with the world, no matter how bad things became, I always knew I would find a way to heal, which allowed me to feel love, compassion and understanding for myself and others. God gifted me with this ability, however as I grew older I started to move away from people and felt uncomfortable with them. I felt so different and felt that nobody understood me or noticed my beautiful soul. I started to become confused and numb as though I didn't know myself anymore. I had lost connection to my soul's love, the spirit within. The words I used to hear from my spirit, 'you are so special Kylie and you are dearly loved, were gone.' I couldn't hear them anymore. Then in May 1994, my life made a complete turn around and finally I found what I had been looking for all my life – unconditional love and my spiritual journey began.

I prayed to God for a miracle, to be able to share my deep feelings of love with another, one who would just love me, one that I felt safe with, who also understood my deep feelings of love. God then led me to Jess, my beautiful horse. I always loved horses and animals in general. I felt so at peace with them, like an inner contentment.

I had been looking for a horse for about six months before I found my beautiful Jess. Where I lived, I used to take a walk around the estate and pass a herd of horses in this five acre paddock not far from my home. I used to love watching them gallop as I walked past; they seemed so graceful and free, expressing themselves freely with total acceptance. One day as I was watching the herd graze in the paddock, one horse noticed me and came over to me. It was love at first sight, a love story you only read or dream of. I had put out prayers to God, of what I wished for in a horse and to my surprise in God's ability to deliver my request, she was everything I ever dreamed of and more.

As I was in awe at her beauty, I held out my hand to connect with her. As her nose touched my hand and I smelt her beautiful scent – the beautiful smell horses have (horsey people will understand what I mean) – for others who have not yet smelt a horses scent, I highly recommend a trip to the country to experience it, it's well worth it. I was in love and had finally found what I had been looking for, to share my soul's deepest love with another who also understood and could see my soul as I did hers.

As I looked into her eyes and she into mine, I knew she could see me and feel the deep feelings of love I felt. She could see my need to share these feelings with her and that I trusted her and had not been able to share my soul's deepest love until now. People had always made fun of my deep feelings; I was always told 'you are so sensitive Kylie.'

Now I know that my sensitivity is a gift, without my sensitivity God has gifted me with, I would not be able to understand and communicate with horses as I do. What I once saw as a burden, I

2

was now grateful for the gift and embraced it.

Every day I could not wait to go and see Jess again and connect with her. I felt so at peace with her, a peace and warmth I had never experienced or felt before.

I would feed her some oats over the fence and we developed a bond. One day as I was with her all my prayers were answered. The lady who lived across from the paddock called out to me "she's a nice mare that one." I said in awe, "she is so beautiful, who owns her." The lady replied "my brother, he had just broken her in and turned her out here to be rested." "I think she is for sale." I was so excited; I said "really, she must be worth a lot," thinking I wouldn't be able to afford her. The lady said, "I'm not sure, but I could find out for you." I said "yes please". I was so excited, but didn't want to get my hopes up as I thought she would be too expensive. I prayed to God that she would be mine and if it was God's will, we would be together.

I went down the following day to see the lady and to my great surprise Jess was for sale at a price I could afford. I had been saving for a horse and had this amount of money saved away. I was shocked that such a beautiful horse was so cheap. The lady said she was this price because she came without papers.

Her brother, a horse trainer, had received her for payment for breaking in another horse for his client who bred her. I asked, "Well when can I speak to your brother." She said, "Right now".

Later in life I had experienced that if something is meant to be and it's for your highest good, everything flows and you have an inner knowing that it feels right. This did feel right, so right – I knew Jess and I had something special to give each other, like all relationships do. I was ready for this relationship, with this beautiful animal God had sent me to. It made my heart sing to be with her. I never questioned it and as time went on our relationship grew.

I would learn later why I chose this very rewarding experience and journey of finding my beautiful horse, my true self, my soul and my divine purpose for being here.

I went to meet the lady's brother who had a horse property just down the road from where I lived. He was a horse trainer and specialized in western riding. He travelled all over the world, entering western competitions and did quite well. As his sister introduced us, he seemed quite charming and business like. He said, "This mare you are interested in has very good blood lines, she is a warmblood." I have always been a kind and honest person, who is a little reserved. I always want to do the best for myself and others, so I said "I haven't been riding for long and I don't know if I'm experienced enough for her."

I loved her so much, I started to feel maybe I wouldn't be able to offer her the best riding experience, allowing her to feel comfortable and enjoy our time together.

He quickly assured me that she was a quiet horse and that he had already had beginners on her and she went quite well. He said "you look like a kind person and I want her to go to a good home." Even though I thought this could have been a bit of a sales pitch, I realised he did seem genuine and he could have sold her very easily.

I said confidently "I can have riding lessons to become a good rider for her." He smiled and said "yes of course". It was meant to be. I think that if something is meant to be, it will be.

I brought her and it was the happiest day of my life. I was overwhelmed with feelings of joy, tears swelled up in my eyes due to happy feelings of emotion. I thought *if she gets sick how I am going to take care of her?* It was then I decided to do a horse course on horse management with the University Of Melbourne, Australia. I also started having riding lessons. Where I rode Jess, they had a 20 metre round yard that was partly covered. The arena had high walls surrounding it and I felt very secure riding her there as we got to know each other. It was like taking baby steps until we felt more comfortable with each other.

Like all relationships at the start there is an adjusting and familiarising process that needs to be taken.

I quickly noticed something was wrong when I asked Jess to move forward from my leg. I wasn't wearing spurs at this stage, they didn't seem necessary and I didn't feel comfortable using them on her. I soon found out that Jess had always been ridden with the rider wearing spurs, therefore wasn't used to a rider not wearing spurs.

After she finally moved forward, she dragged my leg along the side of the round yard and I knew something was dreadfully wrong. I was confused at her doing this, as it seemed like she wanted to hurt me. Later when I got home and removed my pants, the skin on my knees was broken and bleeding. I had scars there for months.

As time went on I realised that Jess was

hurting emotionally inside and was trying to tell me and get my attention. She was in drastic need of healing and to be loved and from what I could see; she had been mistreated like many horses. People had taken and demanded from her and never said 'Thank You'. One day when I was watching this person riding and training Jess just before I had purchased her, I noticed when Jess didn't do what the rider wanted her to do; he would turn his spur inward and dig her in the ribs. She knew he was in the wrong, with that she threw herself and him against the wall of the arena. He saw she was upset and she meant business, so he backed off. It makes me question when I see people who think they have control over the horse when they use an aggressive manner, if the horse doesn't like the rider or their manner and the way they are been treated, they will let the rider know. So I question again, who is the one in control?

I believe in this case the horse is and it is up to us to gain the horse's trust and respect. We need to have the horse disciplined and control of the horse through love, compassion and understanding. We need to have the horse listening to us at all times and to respect us as their leader and guide. Horses can be dangerous, so it's important for them to let us be their leader and guide.

The horse is happy for this if they feel safe, secure, loved and protected by us. If we try to control the horse through demand and aggression, they will feel frightened, insecure and unsafe and therefore feel a need to protect themselves, developing behavioural problems. They never want to hurt us, but they may be hurting themselves emotionally or physically and are trying to tell us.

We need to listen to them and watch their body language for their signals. We expect them to listen to us and do what we want to experience with them; they deserve the same in return. It's God's will that we all be treated with respect and that the horse's kindness never be taken for granted. I ask you, would you stay in a relationship where you were being bullied and kicked? If you did choose to stay, at least you have a choice.

Unfortunately the horse doesn't, all horses have is their body language to communicate with us and let us know how they are feeling emotionally or physically. Because they don't have a choice, I ask that they be respected and loved the way they deserve to be, to be treated with kindness, understanding and compassion.

Doesn't that go for all relationships, what we put in we get back. If we love and nurture our relationships with compassion and understanding we will get this back, it's up to us.

My Spirit within guided me to my beautiful horse

I am the light
I am the love
I see my inner beauty
I see my horse's beauty
Love is all around me
My soul knows it
My soul feels it
I become it
I am it
And so shall it be
by
Kylie Maree Dearden

Chapter 2:

How My Horse Helped Me Find My Soul, My Divine Purpose

Ever since I was a little girl, I always felt a connection with animals, horses in particular. I had so many feelings of love for them. When I was with them, I was so at peace. I looked into their eyes, their soul and we both knew the love of God ever so embedded into our being. Every time I saw animals, horses in particular, I just wanted to touch them, love and connect with them, with their soul. It was so pure and innocent like mine.

As I grew older I realised I had a gift. Then my journey began as I was led to books on spirituality and self help, which helped me understand my gift and what I was here to do. What I had to give to humanity and mostly the animal world.

I quickly learnt that I felt understood by horses. I started to question why and was shown by my spirit within that the unconditional love I feel within my heart and soul, the horses also felt and accepted. I could totally be myself with them and felt a special bond and connection with horses in particular.

Then I developed a special connection with my horse Jess. Finally I was able to share my love with another. She totally understood as she felt the same love in her heart and soul. Then our journey together began. Jess offered me unconditional love, a love I could not find anywhere else or with anyone at that time.

It has been 13 years of pure delight and joy; I can honestly say my horse has helped me find

11

more of the love within myself, the love of God. I will always be so grateful to her for that. I also thank Louise L Hay, as through Louise's books, you can heal your life. I began to release the negative patterns of the past that I was holding onto and was unaware of the effect it was having on my life. It was Louise's books that made me aware that I can create a loving fulfilled life. I spent several years studying spirituality and attending spiritual development classes, meditation and yoga. I learnt how to connect with my soul's love and was guided to my life's purpose.

I am now a qualified Reiki II practitioner in natural healing. A qualified EA NCAS coach and horse instructor, helping horse and rider become one in harmony. Healing comes so naturally to me. I have given several healing treatments to horses and found the responses so rewarding. To see the peace on the horse's faces and to receive the beautiful words, I channel through from spirit to the horse has been such an inspirational experience for me.

I take any opportunity to bring healing and peace to horses, for my spirit within tells me how much they need to be healed for giving so much to us without sometimes getting back the love they need. Not only what they give to humanity, but also the healing they bring to the planet.

As time went on I discovered every horse responded to me in the same way my horse did, kissing me with their muzzle and (nuzzling me). They wanted to connect with me, my soul and my loving energy.

Then I started receiving information from my spirit within. I started to tune into the horses, feelings and emotions. I was tuning into their energy field. I felt their pain, their cries and their sadness. They were all so misunderstood.

Some people were unaware of how horses are such emotional, sensitive animals and I needed to let people know this. The horse also mirrors our thoughts and feelings back to us via their body language. The horse communicates their feelings and emotions this way to get our attention. When I think back to when I was a little girl, I always knew how they felt.

As I developed my spiritual gifts and studied horses more, I began to realise why I have such a strong understanding of them. I noticed how at peace their natural state was, how they just accepted everything and how they don't like fearful situations or negativity. I noticed how graceful and beautiful they were just being and who were so contented with this fact. They ask for little and give so much.

All they want is to be loved, to love, connect and bond with us. They enjoyed been peaceful. This is when I understood their innocence, like mine, they never wanted to hurt anyone, just love them.

Jess helped me connect to my soul

We are what we think
All that we are
arises with our
thoughts
With our thoughts
we make the world
by
Dhammapada

Chapter 3:

Thoughts, How They Create Negative and Positive Experiences with our Horses

As I look back at the 13 years of having my horse, I see at every stage she was mirroring back to me my consciousness (thoughts) of what I believed I deserved and expected at that time, through situations with her that happened. Realising this was a breakthrough for me; I could change my consciousness (thoughts and beliefs). I had the power within me to do this and I knew our life would become more joyful and harmonious. So about 11 years ago, I began to study thoughts and how they shape our experiences and our lives. Every time we think a thought or speak a word the Universe is listening and responding to us. The relationship we have with horses reflects back to us our current thoughts and beliefs. I remember years ago when I took my horse to her first show.

At the time I did not respect myself and my horse reflected this back to me. She kicked out at me during the led class trying to get my attention. She did not like the show rides that were close to where our led class was and neither did I, but instead of listening to her and my intuition and leaving the show grounds, I allowed my ego (trying to prove something) to ignore her hints and forced myself and her into staying. My ego was in charge and I had disconnected from my soul. It was not safe for me to have her in this environment –I was expecting too much from her. As I began changing my thinking and words I spoke, my experiences also changed. As I started to respect myself more, so did my horse. I was opening my heart to allow the love in, I was beginning to heal and my horse was my best guide and teacher to how much I was healing and how much I had healed. She would show me when I was coming from love or fear by how she was responding to me. I was so grateful to her for this guidance. No matter how difficult our lives are, we can make positive changes today. We can get control back of our lives as we become aware of our thoughts and begin to change them from negative to positive. Positive loving thoughts create positive results and negative fearful thoughts create negative experiences and responses from our horses. Thoughts are energy and energy travels from us to our horse no matter where we are. I could be at home thinking about my horse and if I am thinking loving peaceful thoughts about her, she is going to sense and feel this energy I am sending her. Hence if I have negative thoughts such as demand, lack, resentment, guilt, fear and so on towards her, she will also sense and feel this.

She knows demand is not love and she only responds back to me what I give her, in my actions, words, thoughts and emotions I have towards her and life. Many of us are not aware of how energy works and how we are all connected to it. It's not something we learnt at school or from our parents.

It's not until we are open and we begin to learn and be led to this important and vital information that sets us free, from past limitations and allows us to find harmony within ourselves and our horse right now in the present moment by simply being willing to change our thoughts. We seem to be always living in our past. What we are living in this moment is what we have created from our past thoughts and beliefs. If there is something going on in our lives that we don't like, we have the option of re-creating our experiences for the future. I remember one place I was agisting my horse, she kept getting out of the fences to the grass in the laneway. The fence was electric but she knew that with her rugs on, she could lie down and wriggle her way underneath without getting a shock. Mind you there was quite a space between the last line of the fencing to the ground for her to be able to get out. I advised the owners at the time that were already aware of her getting out and were going to fix the fencing.

As time went on the owners of the property were busy with other things going on and Jess continued to get out into the laneway. I even saw her wriggle under the fence and get out into the laneway one day when I had just arrived.

What I failed to see until I moved her to another agistment, was that Jess was showing me I needed to set boundaries in my life with what I was willing to accept as a good and safe enough environment for her to live in.

I wanted Jess to live in a safe, secure environment with clear boundaries set as to what I would accept and what I considered dangerous and not safe. I wanted the owners of the property to care for the well being and safety of the horse like I did.

With this new awareness and grateful for this insight Jess was showing me, I started to set clear boundaries to people in my life on how I expected myself and Jess to be treated. I started to expect more for myself and her, asking the Universe to bring in lots of loving, kind likeminded people into our lives. I put out a request to the Universe for a safe place for Jess to live in, a secure environment with loving owners and all the things Jess and I required, at a price I could afford. I found just the place and thanked the Universe for guiding me there. As we begin to change our thinking, we may not see many positive results right away, but as we continue with our new thought patterns, we will find every new day becoming different. Once we believe we deserve the best, we will find it and see it in our lives. If we want to have more positive experiences in our lives, then we must change our thinking today.

Today's thoughts create our experiences in the days to come. So moment by moment we are consciously or unconsciously choosing healthy (positive) or unhealthy (negative) thoughts.

These thoughts affect our bodies and our horses as we connect to our horses via our thoughts, be it negatively or positively, hopefully positive for your own well being and ultimately our horses.

I have used affirmations daily for years now. I just love them; they make me feel good about myself. I recommend any of Louise L Hay's books or positive thought cards. I have found them best for me, but any positive affirmations are good. Choose which ever ones feel right for you. You'll know I just found Louise's to resonate with me; she has such a loving nurturing manner about her and the way her affirmations are written.

You feel her love and for me she has been a guiding light. I needed her love and I felt her approval of me as I would read her books. Louise gave this healing information so freely, knowing she would connect to your soul and I knew that if I would open my heart and soul to her words of peace, love and self approval that I would feel good. It takes commitment and dedication with affirmations before you really start to see the results. For me it's a life change and I love it. I realised if I was going to offer myself and my horse the best life possible then I needed to invest lots of time into reprogramming my mind.

By releasing negative thoughts I received and replacing them with positive ones, I began to see the joy it brought into my life. This is an ongoing process and one I am fully committed to and hope you are too.

You and your horse are worth it. I believe until you start having loving thoughts towards yourself and your horse, you will not find harmony with them. Once we find harmony within ourselves, we will then find harmony with our horses. Good luck and remember we are all following the same journey to self love and approval. Your horse and the universal intelligence (God, spirit, and soul) – whatever you believe in, will show you the way. Follow your heart – there is no blame, there is however a new moment and that moment is now.

What thought are you having right now? Is it a loving thought towards yourself and your horse and is it serving yourself and your horse's highest good. What you think and do for your horse's highest good, you in turn are doing the best for your highest good and all of humanity. We are all one and connected to the universal intelligence (God, energy, white light). So the more we think loving towards ourselves and others, the more we heal the planet and everything in it.

Now if that isn't a good enough reason to be more loving in all that we do, then I don't know what else there is. To me there is only one way and that way is to love one another.

Keeping our thoughts positive creates positive experiences with our horses

I am worthy of
Divine love
I deserve it
I experience it
I feel it
and
I accept it
now
by
Kylie Maree Dearden

Chapter 4:

Developing the Relationship with Yourself

Our parents bring us into the world and we love them for doing the best they can, bringing us up with the knowledge and understanding they had at that time. I believe we all have lessons to learn from our parents. For me, and I believe for all of us on some level, we are to learn from our parents, to find the love of self. Our parents can't find our soul's love (God's love) within ourselves for us. We come through them, not of them (as quoted in The Prophet by Kahlil Gibran a fantastic inspiring book to read). We are to release the need of our parent's approval and accept ourselves for who we are, perfect whole and complete, right here, right now. Our parents, like us, are also on a spiritual journey. Like us they are finding their love within themselves more and more through life's experiences. Everything in life mirrors back to us what we believe about ourselves and what we deserve. Learning this and becoming aware of how the Universe works, we are able to change ourselves and the way we think. This changes the experiences we have in life.

As we start to become aware of the thoughts we think and if we have negative thoughts about ourselves or others such as criticism or judgment, we realise this is not serving our highest good, nor is it creating wonderful experiences for ourselves and others. As I practiced yoga and meditation, my mind started to become quiet and I realised these critical thoughts about myself and others were not mine. They were all programming I had taken in from my past and I realised they were other people's thoughts of me that I had taken on as mine. This was such a breakthrough for me as I knew I had the power to change these thoughts and become the person I knew I already was. The funny thing was as I started to release old limiting thoughts and replace them with more loving, kind thoughts of myself, I started to see my true self emerge like a butterfly from its cocoon. I realised that I had always been this person; it's just that I had lost touch with my soul's love. I started to see that I always had these loving thoughts as a child and especially about animals and horses in general and how powerful they made me feel. They understand me and I them, we were looking for the same thing. God took me to horses to help me find God's love in my heart and soul.

I started to see that as I spent time with my horse and by myself, I was able to easily access my soul's love and something inside me said give yourself time to be on your own, to find out why this is happening. So I did the most liberating thing I ever did, which as a result gave me freedom. I got right into personal development and attended spiritual development classes for years and loved it. I took charge of my life and reprogrammed my mind. I released all of the harmful thoughts and replaced them with good thoughts about myself and others.

As time went on and I became more confident, I noticed people becoming uncomfortable around me and they started to leave my life. I had this strong desire within me to achieve and accomplish a great goal in this life. I felt this force within me stronger and stronger and it was guiding me every step of the way. I felt protected, safe and loved.

I knew I was doing the right thing for myself and others. I believe this force within was and still is my spirit (universal energy, white light and love of God) that is within all of us and created everything including us.

I soon noticed that new positive people entered my life at anytime I needed encouragement and guidance to confirm what I felt. The spirit within led me to people and situations that would confirm I was on the right path for me. My life became an exciting journey of self discovery. I started to be so grateful for all my relationships and I could see that if there was anything I was uncomfortable about in another, it was something I must be uncomfortable about within me. So I would embrace whatever it was and I found more love and light within my soul as a result of this. I do believe that it is a journey to connecting to the spirit within, our soul's love, a lifetime journey.

Relationships are here to help us grow and find more of that light and love within ourselves. Once we see life through these beautiful eyes we are free. We are living the love of God. We will shine like a beacon and light the way for others. We begin to realise that we are the ones in control of manifesting our future. I highly recommend you read *"The Power of Intention"* by Dr Wayne W. Dyer. God led me to Dr Wayne W. Dyer's books to help me understand what I was experiencing and it did just that.

God bless Dr Wayne W. Dyer. I also recommend positive affirmations to be practiced, as well as yoga and meditation daily. This will not only help you with your riding but helps to access your higher self – your love and spirit within. If you have never practiced meditation, its ok, it takes time. It's not going to happen overnight. Even just some relaxation breathing is good if that's all you can manage. I assure you the benefits are very rewarding and well worth it. For me it gave a sense of inner peace, direction and eventually led me to my divine purpose. Also you need to send forgiveness to yourself and others. Have loving kind thoughts towards everyone and everything. Know that you are doing the best you can and so are they. Try to focus on the good in all no matter what. Forgive all, for we are all travelling this spiritual journey in a physical body. Do not judge others, for you will be judged. As I see others face difficulties with their horses, I remember I too was once there. I too had to experience to understand. I too was offered love and forgiveness by the Great Spirit. We are to offer this to others. God does not want us to take on board another's pain or lesson they need to learn but I can send them love, peace and compassion. As you find the love of God within yourself, you will see your horse mirror back to you this love. I guarantee it. My beautiful horse does and I feel the blissful universal energy of love flow through me every time I'm with her. It moves me and I know at that space and time I am being loved the way God intended me to be and tears of joy well up in my eyes as I say a prayer of thanks to my creator and Jess for allowing me to experience for what I call, 'Heaven on Earth'.

We owe it to
our horses
to connect to
the spirit within
We owe it
to ourselves
by
Kylie Maree Dearden

Chapter 5:

Connecting to Our Soul's Love, The Spirit Within

By connecting to our soul's love, our inner being and spirit within, we will also connect to our horse's soul and share a wonderful relationship for a lifetime. We owe it to our horses and all animals to love and appreciate them –we owe it to ourselves. Horses, more than dogs and other animals, suffer more emotional and physical pain. We have a different relationship with a horse than we do a dog. When we sit on our horses, we connect to its energy field and it connects with ours. That is why it is so important to come from love, kindness and a positive manner towards our horses. The more positive and loving we are, the more the horse will respond to us positively and lovingly. The more we focus on keeping our thoughts positive, the better our relationship with them will be.

As I continued to become aware and focus on my negative thoughts and replaced them with positive loving thoughts, with the help of Louise L Hay's book, I felt my soul's love begin to deepen more and more. I've always been a very loving person and tried to bring light and love to all I come into contact with.

During my meditations one day about 10 years ago, I realised I had discovered 'divine love of self' and that through staying connected to my soul's love when interacting with horses and people, I was also connecting with their soul's love. As my mind would go quiet and I studied spiritually more, I had so many wonderful experiences with

31

spirit – the universal energy (white light).

As I built my energy up more and more, I became more confident and comfortable. It got to the stage where I felt so much love and joy in my heart and soul. This blissful energy would flow through my body, leaving me in awe and speechless. I found myself in a state of blissfulness often and was fascinated by it. I was so grateful to be experiencing it and had to find out more about it. I knew it was God's love, the universal energy of the divine, but what was it trying to tell me?

I started to experience this blissful energy flow through my body when people spoke to me about things they wanted to do in their lives. I also felt this blissful energy when people would talk about their loved ones who had passed over. Then certain music would resonate with me, each song had a special meaning at that time in my life.

While I was in meditation one day, I asked 'Great Spirit you have given me so much love in my heart and soul, all of my life I knew you were there, what would you have me do with this beautiful gift you have bestowed upon me?' I was guided, 'teach other's to find their soul's love as you have found me, for I am always there in all hearts and souls.' I accepted this wonderful gift gracefully.

As I started to do the work of God in all that I do, as I believe we are all meant to do, my life become so rewarding. I received love from almost all people and all animals I came into contact with.

If I am ever having a frustrated moment, I quickly see it's because I am not loving myself enough, so off I go to do some affirmations and connect back to my soul's love. As I come across people or horses that are upset or sad, I try to listen and comfort them; offering them my compassion and understanding and allowing them to connect back to their soul's love again.

I believe we need to develop a relationship with ourselves first and find our soul's love before we can receive love back. It's simple – what you give out, you get back. Therefore, we need to be careful what thoughts we are putting out. We need to release all negative thoughts of lack, limitation, fear, resentment and anger and replace them with thoughts of joy, happiness and love. Horses are great teachers and healers for this self awareness process that we all must go through. Horses mirror back to you your thoughts and feelings, as well as their own. Your feelings and emotions move through your body to your horse.

How ironic, horses pick up on these emotions and feelings and mirror them back to us to look at and deal with. In fact all relationships are about growth within ourselves, offering us a wonderful opportunity to grow.

I find horses in particular offer you unconditional love while you go through this healing and growing process. They don't have an agenda, unless it's how to get another carrot, but really how harmless. It would take a really angry horse to try to hurt you physically. If this is the case they must have been hurt and abused in their past and are suffering. All this negativity we receive from the horse generally has been given to them from past human interaction.

Everything we are is a product of what we have experienced from our environment while growing up. We can seek help and change, where horses are at our mercy.

That's why it's our responsibility to become more joyful and peaceful once we heal from our past pain and take ownership. These messages we have that are negative and hurtful are from past programmed memories that our mind has remembered and believes to be true.

Our soul never gives us negative messages; it always speaks words of love and truth, giving us a feeling of joy and happiness, peace and harmony. It never criticizes, only encourages our strengths and helps us to see our weaknesses. It doesn't want us to give power to them but simply allows us to see the weaknesses and move through them in love.

As I sit connected to my soul's love, I think of loving thoughts of horses and animals in general. I'm so grateful to God for creating such wonderful animals that I am able to share myself with.

My horse never takes advantage of me or takes me for granted, nor do I her. No matter how many times I tell her she is a beautiful girl, who I dearly love and appreciate, she never gets tired of hearing it or feels uncomfortable. She just responds with more love. It amazes me. While I share my loving thoughts with her and the feelings I have for her, I express it because it makes my heart sing with joy and comes so natural to me. I know I am pleasing God, the spirit within. I know this is God's will on how she is to be treated and loved. I don't expect anything back from her. I do it for the joy of giving, service to God. I find horses are very open to being loved. Keeping my thoughts loving allows me to experience these joyful moments with my horse all of the time.

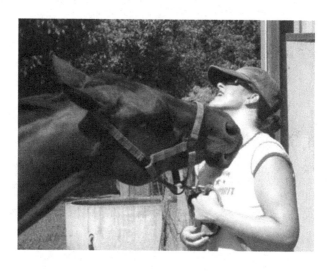

Jess helped me connect to my soul's love

Dearest friend
I salute the divinity
within you
I honour you
I serve you
For your
unconditional love
forever more
Your friend always
Kylie
by
Kylie Maree Dearden

Chapter 6:

Understanding Your Horse Emotionally and Spiritually

Horses are very sensitive spiritual animals, they know they are already perfect – whole and complete, just as they are. They accept themselves totally; they know they are unique, graceful and loved by the universal intelligence. They know they are here to love us unconditionally as God gifted them with this ability. We think we teach horse's things and we do, but they teach us something much more than we could ever teach them. They teach us to love and accept ourselves if we are open to seeing this. I believe we interact with horses to find unconditional love that we may have never had or felt before. We are unaware that we may be dependent on our horses emotionally for this love we may never have received. We may have unresolved anger, resentment and take this out on our horses at times. No matter how many times it takes us to realise this and to become aware, our horse still loves us and wants to be our friend.

They can feel our pain and they take it in their stride, or mirror it back to us to deal with. Yet if we ask ourselves honestly, if we treated a friend the way that I see some horses being treated, they would no longer want to be our friend and can you blame them? Lucky for our friends they can walk away, our horses can't.

Our horses have to stay and suffer in pain the lack of emotional and spiritual love that they need. Alternatively, it is you who can set your horse free and yourself by becoming aware and changing the way you treat your horse from fear – ego, to love – light. Horses are no different from us as regards to emotions and feelings. All they want is to enjoy their relationship with us and to be respected, appreciated and yes – loved. Just like we like to be treated, God gifted horses with a very kind and gentle heart and soul and because of this gentleness they possess, they seek security from us. They respect us as the leader, if we earn their respect. This does not give us reason to think we have the right to overpower them in a cruel way, for this is not love. To be able to interact with them is a gift. A gift that we should respect, honour and never taken advantage of. I know whenever my horse is unsure of anything, she looks at me in a certain way and says to me with her body language, 'I am frightened Kylie' and I say 'yes I know sweetie, there is nothing to be frightened of here, trust me, you are safe with me. I will love, protect and serve you.' I then stoke her along the neck; she feels my calmness, reassurance and trusts me that I will protect her. It's only the horses that don't feel safe and protected that develop all sorts of emotional behaviour problems, which can lead to many unnecessary bad experiences for all horses and riders. I can't stress enough how important it is to reassure your horse at these times they feel insecure.

Horses aren't fussed with fancy rugs; they want to be groomed all over and talked to, which makes them feel calm, safe and loved. They need you to speak words of reassurance to them when they feel frightened, not to be kicked in the gut and punished for their instinctual state of flight with unfamiliar things. If you were upset about something and confused, I'm sure you would want someone to listen to how you feel. Horses are just the same emotionally. They need to know you enjoy spending time with them, other than just riding them.

They need to connect with you on a soul level if they are to be totally balanced emotionally and spiritually. I know my horse loves to connect and bond with me on a regular basis. This is especially important for horses that are kept in a yard on their own. Horses need to groom and connect with each other; this gives them a great sense of well being. It's natural for horses to groom and bond with each other for hours at a time in a herd. This is very comforting and has great healing and therapeutic benefits for your horse's emotional well being. People say that a horse is happiest out to pasture in a herd, but I feel they have adjusted to this life with us and accepted it. I know my horse loves my company and interaction with humans, she tells me so. Even when I first met her, she was the only one in the herd who came up to me to say 'hello, let's be friends.' She knew we had a lot to share and give each other. She was looking for security and she knew I could offer her this.

When I first brought her, I was going through a difficult time in my life. One day when I went down to check on her, she was trotting around annoying the other horses, as I had her in a herd at this time. On this day I couldn't catch her, she seemed to be lost and confused.

Now I look back, I see she was mirroring my consciousness at the time. I was also lost and confused and trying to find my way. Later, as my spiritual gifts developed, I started to understand her body language and what she was trying to say to me by tuning into her energy field, her feelings and emotions. Horses look for security in humans to look after them and make them feel safe. They need to connect to the human on a soul level, to know they are loved and protected. Horses as a herd animal do not enjoy being on the run all the time as in the wild. They wish to be at peace just like we do. We can offer each other a great gift, which is why I believe God brought us together – to love one another. Horses need to know that you are not just interested in taking from them but are also willing to give. As they do unconditionally, this comes naturally to them as sometimes we seem to struggle to practice this unconditional love in our relationships. I believe horses teach us to love unconditionally, if we want to learn. I myself have to admire and honour horses for this; for they are my greatest teachers. God bless them.

I choose to serve horses for a lifetime because of their ability to love us unconditionally and for all they have taught me. This does not mean that we need to be hard on ourselves if we are having a frustrated moment. We simply need to walk away from our horses at this time, until we have calmed down before approaching them again.

Otherwise they will feel our change in energy and start to become unsettled and possibly frustrate you even more. Also, don't be afraid to talk to them, they love it. Tell them you are sorry and how you feel – trust me they hear and understand every word you say and feel every feeling you feel. They are very forgiving and the best listeners.

My horse nudges me on my arm very gently

and says, 'it's ok Kylie I understand, I still love and appreciate you, for looking after me and for loving me.' By being open with your feelings and acknowledging them, you are freeing yourself of them and your horse is more than willing to listen and understand. Try it the next time you are upset – tell your horse how you feel. I promise your horse will not judge you and it will bring you closer together. By ignoring your feelings and those of your horse, you are denying both of you a chance to bond and heal if necessary. We are all learning and growing – that's the journey of life. Through our relationships, we are offered the wonderful opportunity to grow spiritually into a more loving person each day. So next time you see your horse, try opening your heart to it. Your horse is always ready and waiting to embrace the light that shines from your soul. I know it's there and so does your horse. Try it; you'll be amazed and delighted at the welcome response, when you say to your horse: 'Hello my beautiful one, how are you feeling today?' your horse will respond with, 'hello my dear friend, finally you have found the light of your soul, I'm so glad. Now we can share the kind of loving relationship, God intended us to have and we can leave all that other negative, fearful stuff behind us that did not serve either or us any good.'

Jess and I playing and having fun – this helps your horse stay happy emotionally and spiritually

Jess
You are my beloved
My true companion
As I look into
your eyes
I see the light
of your soul
and
it touches me so
by
Kylie Maree Dearden

Chapter 7:

Developing the Relationship & Bond with My Horse

When I first brought my horse, it took me one year to regain her trust. She had lost faith in humans and their ability to love her the way she deserved, the way God had intended. She knew the people that had been riding her were in a great deal of emotional pain and they took it out on her. She was tired and just wanted to be loved. As I spent time with her, I soon noticed she had developed a defence mechanism towards me. This was due to the way she had been handled in the past. She would anticipate I was going to mistreat her and she would clam up to protect herself from further pain. I also noticed her nervousness as she was tied up, she never seemed to be able to relax and trust that she was safe. I started to wonder what had happened to her as she was tied up. I guess I didn't really need to try and find out, as she told me the whole story by her body language and by tuning into her I soon found out.

I have always had these abilities to feel what the horse is feeling by tuning into their energy and feelings. It's no different than picking up on feelings from our friends and family members.

Most of us do this without even knowing and I believe we all have spiritual gifts and talents. We are all connected to the universal intelligence I call God and we are all able to help one another.

It just depends on the level of understanding that we have and as we develop and grow we are then open to being guided more by this infinite source, for our highest good and that of others.

Twelve months of regaining my horse's trust consisted of a lot of ground work. I love to touch and connect with her. I always have, it's my way of sharing my soul's love. Horses are so connected to the source – God, much more than we are. Being in nature and their hoofs touching the ground helps horses stay in touch with the universal intelligence God. Unlike humans, who have the capability of presumably higher brain functions and something referred to as an ego, which if allowed can convince us that we are disconnected from our source – God. As Jess helped me become aware of my connection to the source – God, by being in her presence, I started to understand myself and her and the beautiful gift we offered to each other. I started to realise why I wanted to spend so much time with her. I felt so good in her presence and even when I got home after being with her. We were healing each other by connecting with our source – God.

We were channelling this healing energy of love through each other which allowed us to release all past pain we had received that was not ours to own, but somehow we had allowed it to be dumped onto us without even realising it.

Now we were both able to heal and move ahead to live a joyful life full of peace, harmony and well being, touching all we come in contact with, this love. Spreading this light to all and reminding them of their divineness. As I went through my healing stage and realised the pain of the past, I noticed Jess offering me an opportunity to listen to her and heal.

For a long time she tried to communicate with me, through her body language and later when I developed my spiritual and physic abilities to tune into their energy field and feelings, I felt the pain in her body. At first I ignored her constant nudges on my arm with her nose. I was always in a rush at these times and said to her, 'yes okay in a minute. She was trying to say to me, 'I love you, I miss you and can I have a pat, a hug and another carrot please, they taste so good.' At the start she wanted to get my attention and I soon realised that she wanted to bond and connect with me. This, she showed me, gave her a feeling of being secure. I now believe the only way we are able to share this special bond with horses is because of their natural instinct to be in a herd, with a leader to warn them of any danger they need to run from.

She was saying to me 'I'm happy for you to be my leader and I need to bond with you and feel connected to you if we are to have this relationship together.' 'So I can feel safe and secure and balanced emotionally.' Now I know when she wants to bond and connect she leans her head over my shoulder and around my neck. I stand there with her just holding her in an embrace. At this time my mind is quiet – blank and at peace.

We both know at that time we are part of each other sharing our soul's love, appreciating the Universe for bringing us together to share this great love and never taking it for granted. I feel so overwhelmed with joyful emotions at these times and say prayers to God and Jess just listens and touches me with her nose ever so gently to confirm that she feels the same. I also know the times when I just go down to feed her and pick up the manure in her paddock. As I leave she stomps her hoof on the ground and turns around to face me.

Sometimes she shakes her head in disapproval of me leaving her so soon. I check to see there are no flies or insects that may be upsetting her. During winter I can't use the flies or insects as an excuse. I tell her that I dearly love her and tomorrow we will bond and have a ride together. I noticed she was happier with me telling her I will be back tomorrow; she is calm when I leave. By me listening to her feelings we have a closer and more harmonious relationship, by me communicating to her in a loving way, she was more at peace. I noticed a big change in her as I started to do this every time I saw her. I told her everything we were going to do.

I would tell her roughly what time I would be back and if I needed someone else I trusted to feed her, I would tell her I was still her owner and she was dearly loved. I would leave her saying, 'you take care of yourself my beautiful girl, you are safe and protected here and you know you are always with me in spirit. I would never leave you sweetie and I love you so much.' As I gave my horse this reassurance, she started to relax more, her behaviour totally changed.

When I would leave her she had this peacefulness about her – I was amazed at her response. Horses love it when you talk to them in a calm, soothing voice. It comforts them and interests them; they feel included in what you are doing and feel happy and content. They get bored being in the paddock sometimes and love to hear what you have to say, it brings entertainment to their day. I realise she is much happier when I tell her what I'm doing, where I am going and when I will be back. If we are going to build a relationship and bond with our horses, I believe it is our responsibility to prepare them and acknowledge their feelings, their being. This is what they require from us because they have accepted us as their leader.

They look to us for this reassurance that they are loved, protected and safe. We are never to take advantage of their ability to love unconditionally and if we do, we will pay the consequences. To protect themselves horses will play up and build barriers, they will mirror back to us via their body language and feelings, how we are treating them.

Most times unintentionally, we will take this reaction from them out on them again. It becomes a vicious cycle, until eventually the horse's spirit dies within. These are the horses you see where they are here in the physical body, but not here in spirit. They stand there switched off, aloof, vague and in extreme cases come towards you with anger and possibly bare their teeth at you, kick you, or bite you. These horses are in desperate need of healing, most likely from having been confused in the present and past. We can only attract to us in the horse what we need to know about ourselves and the horse. This insight and awareness gives you and your horse both a chance to heal and build a loving relationship.

Developing the relationship and bond with Jess- a necessary element to finding harmony with your horse

Dearest one
As I touch you
and
stroke
your beautiful mane
I feel your spirit
It's so pure
We become one
Connecting in wholeness
That is
a gift
from God
by
Kylie Maree Dearden

Chapter 8:

Connecting with Your Horse Spiritually

Once you have connected to the spirit within and you are coming from love towards your horse instead of ego, your horse will become more relaxed and feel safe and protected. As I have observed my horse I have noticed at the times I have become disconnected to my soul, my source – God, that Jess has become very unsettled. As I connected back to my soul (my source – God), she was relaxed again. Sometimes when life's issues arise, we naturally – being human – become confused and frightened or anxious. As we become aware of how this affects our horses, we can take action to eliminate the negative thoughts and fear by having positive loving thoughts. I read positive affirmations – they are a wonderful tool to use at these difficult times in our spiritual growth and journey. They help me connect back to my spirit within. It's so important to try and stay connected to our spirit as much as we can. Our horses see us as the leader and they rely on us so much for guidance. If we become anxious or frightened, they think there is something to worry about too. They feel our negative fearful energy and start to panic and feel insecure. This is how horses react, in a herd, if the leader shows the other horses their frightened, the other horses will respond and follow – flee. They put their trust into their leader to guide them to safety. Seen as we are the leader's now, it's our responsibility to guide and protect our horse's.

This means by staying connected to our soul

and spirit within. Now it may take time before you feel the universal energy flowing through your body as I do when I ride my horse, but it is possible to achieve. With focused intention and self awareness, I found it and I believe you can too. It's worth it, having meditated for years and releasing negative thought patterns that entered my mind and replacing them with positive loving thoughts, I am now a clear channel for spirit to work through me most of the time. The more our thoughts vibrate at a higher level of love and kindness, the more this higher energy of the Universe can flow through us, uplifting us and connecting horse and rider together to become one. I know Jess feels my thoughts all the time and I choose to focus on positive loving ones and I always see great results. I believe in myself and her to be able to achieve anything together we desire. For me, it's riding together in peace and harmony at all times. I can honestly say we have achieved this but only by staying connected to the source and our soul's love. My horse has been willing and open to share this experience with me. Once you reach this level, it is very rewarding, however it does take a lot of work. I'm always taking time to look at myself within, my inner self – it's a wonderful thing. By doing this it gives you a chance to change anything that is creating disharmony within yourself and your horse. It's a never ending journey of self discovery, from releasing doubtful chit chat that our mind keeps playing over and over again and again, of the past. Through self awareness and dedication we can change it.

I have and it has taken years but that's the exciting journey and your horse will love you every step of the way. Mine did and I know yours will too, so next time you're being hard on yourself, or your horse, ask yourself, what is it I'm trying to achieve here?

Whatever it is, tell yourself you can let it go and turn to your horse and give them a big hug and tell them how much you love and appreciate them for their patience and understanding. Then try to be more patient with yourself and others. We aren't expected to know it all, in fact we can't, there will always be more to learn every day. It's God's will we stay open to a better way, a more loving way, that's all. The rewards are more love in return and most of all more peace and harmony for you and your horse. This I know to be true, in my purest moments with spirit, this is what I feel. I trust this part of myself that guides me into doing what's right for my horse and other horses, it's a feeling I get. Trust that feeling and intuition guiding you and your horse. It will never lie to you. If something doesn't feel right, listen to this feeling. Change instructor or trainers if their methods don't feel right to you. Change your approach if necessary and seek help if you're not sure. Your heart will tell you and when you ask the Universe for what you want, it will guide you to who you need to see to help you and it will feel right. It's when we ignore these messages from God that we fall into trouble. Remember, there is always a solution to every problem if you believe there is and the Universe will find a way to bring it to you. Have faith and remember everything happens for the best, whether it's good or bad, it's all for a reason and your growth. Every situation good or bad brings you closer to the light within.

I believe all situations are for the good and if it feels bad, I believe it is God's way of showing you that something better is needed here and is coming your way. This I am certain of because it has always happened in my life. Every negative experience I have had has brought me closer towards finding the light within me and peace and harmony have been the rewards. At times when I have been riding my horse and fear has crept in, usually from me, I bring my horse back to a walk and take a few deep breaths. If I still feel nervous, I take another few deep breaths until I connect back to the source again and feel peace and harmony flowing through me. I also affirm I am at peace and totally safe and protected at all times. If I still feel nervous and my horse is starting to react, I get off her and lunge her or continue my training another day. My intuition usually lets me know if it's safe for us to continue. Sometimes you will find it challenging when you are riding with other people. I try as much as possible to ride on my own, as I want to achieve quality training and riding with my horse. However, it is good practice to ride with others, especially if you are competing as you will need to ride with other horse and riders around you. Just try to stay centered in peace and love and stay away from riders and horses who you don't feel safe around. People have different methods of training and riding their horses. We are only ever to do what feels right for us. I'll never forget the time I was riding my horse, when a girl decided to lunge her horse in the arena at the same time.

That was fine, but the problem was she had forgot to bring her lunging whip, so instead found this pole with a plastic bag attached to the end of it that was used for free jumping the horse to stay on the course. Every time she waved the pole, the plastic bag naturally made a loud noise, as you can imagine. Jess became unsettled and was looking at the girl trying to figure out what she was doing and was she going to come after her next with this plastic bag that made a horrible noise to my horse's sensitive ears.

I could see Jess was no longer relaxed and was not going to learn anything. So I decided to walk Jess calmly around one end of the arena and practiced some other things at the walk. I then decided it was a waste of time for me to ride my horse, as she was learning nothing except for how to become unsettled. My horse was younger back then and we were still building trust, nowadays we don't have a problem. I just go far enough away or ride outside somewhere safe and I hope you do too if you ever come across this situation. For me there is a right time and method to introduce plastic bags to your horse so they aren't frightened of them and for me this was not the right time or method I would use. There will be times when you will have to decide if it is safer to stay or go. Choose what feels right at the time and try to stay connected to your source – God, the spirit within at all times. You have nothing to prove to yourself and every reason to think of your own and your horse's safety at all times. You can't be responsible for other people's choices or energies they choose to be part of. You can only be responsible for yourself and whenever something like this happens, I see it's the Universe's way of getting my attention. I have attracted this situation to me and if I choose to show that person love, compassion and understanding that is the highest good for all concerned and in those situations that's what I feel I am to do.

Jess and I becoming one in harmony – mentally, emotionally, physically and spiritually

Always
train your
horse
with love
Feel it
Become it
Express it
and
Be it
by
Kylie Maree Dearden

Chapter 9:

Training Your Horse Spiritually

When we train our horses from an ego and a forceful approach this shows our horses there is a lack of respect for the horse – it's like we believe that the horse is beneath us and that because we are human, we have the right to overpower them with force, brutality and disrespect of the sorts. To avoid pain, the horse will submit through fear of being hurt. This is where the horse develops behavioural problems and some horses who don't submit become unable to be trained and unmanageable or uncontrollable. These horses are not willing to put up with this kind of training method and treatment and can you blame them? I have proved, like many, that you don't need to use force or brutality to train and ride a horse. Now, I'm the first to admit horses are huge powerful animals which need to be taught to respect you and your space and they must have set boundaries and be clear on these to be safe for all. However, there is a big difference between kind discipline to forced discipline. I have noticed horses that have chosen to submit due to fear to avoid pain have become what I call 'numb.' As I approach the horse, it is switched off – I can tell through looking into its eyes, observing its facial expressions and tuning into its energy field.

I believe to protect itself from further pain, the horse puts up walls and barriers and becomes depressed, which then leads to behavioural problems. We are responsible for this happening and what's a concern is how we treat others we treat ourselves. We all deserve to be loved, nurtured, respected and appreciated for our efforts; this is true for all of us. I know horses sometimes, like ourselves, just have a bad day, they may be feeling tired or stiff etc. This is the time we need to be understanding and show compassion towards our horses. Just as they offer this to us while we are learning how to ride better and to understand what they need from us. I know with my horse when she comes into season, she becomes a little restless and all her hormones are going wild. I understand that with her being a mare; she is going through cycles, experiencing different emotions and physical changes within her. At these times I offer her empathy and understanding. I simply react to her with love at all times now and have noticed she feels my calmness and this helps her relax. If I reacted in an abrupt, controlling way to her at these times, it would make it worse – she would tense up even more. If I was to react to her harshly and try to punish her for this restlessness she would become upset and our time together would become unpleasant. If we are training the horse something and it doesn't respond the way we would like it to, I calmly ask it again and sometimes you have to be firm but never in a manner that frightens or abuses the horse. This will cause the horse to remember a bad experience with you and prevent you both from moving forward together. Sometimes it takes a while for the horse to understand what we are teaching them. Or something could be wrong with our horse, mentally, emotionally, physically or spiritually.

The more our horse trusts us and feels comfortable, the more they will learn, grow and most importantly relax and enjoy the experience with us.

Try putting yourself in their position, how would you like to be treated? By being given the gift to be able to interact with these wonderful animals, we need to appreciate anything they offer us, know matter how small it is. They have the right to say 'no, I don't want to do that, it doesn't feel right to me.' Just like we have the choice to not want to do something we don't like or doesn't feel right to us. They deserve the same respect and choices. I have seen that if you love them, they will offer you what you want and much more. I would never have believed that I would have received the responses and love that my horse has shown me through loving her. She still amazes me today, more and more. The more I learn to love myself and her, the more she mirrors that love back to me. My priorities were my horse's wellbeing and happiness and still are. This was at the top of my list. I was grateful for this awareness and the peace that I felt from it.

I started to realised no amount of money could ever give me the love I feel in my heart and soul when I connect with horses. I feel this blissful energy of spirit when I am with them and healing them, it's so rewarding for me. To be able to give them any kind of peace and harmony is a great gift to me. I know I love them the way God does and I am serving and honouring them the way God intended. How could one not feel fulfilled when all you do in every interaction with them is give and exchange love?

Horses truly amaze me, no matter how they have been treated in the past. They always welcome me and are very open to the love I offer them.

This trait I admire and honour as to me they are great spiritual teachers and with this I felt they should be respected for this at all times and that I should never take advantage of them. This is a gift they have, an ability to love unconditionally. I see them as my teachers, not me as their teacher. They help me grow to be the best I can towards myself, them and other people I come in contact with. I realised a long time ago why I loved horses so much and was so attracted to their beauty and grace. One time I was going through a big spiritual growth within myself and I became a little frustrated. Things were not going well in my life and I could not see at the time my horse was trying to love me and help me release my pain and hurt. She had been spiritually connected to me and all of a sudden felt disconnected from me. I realised at this time she felt this I had become disconnected to my soul's love by feeling negative and hopeless with feelings of unworthiness. As days went by and I started to heal and open up my heart again, I realised no matter how many times I was going through this phase of difficulties, she still had all this love in her heart for me and she showed it to me all of the time. She was healing me and could see I was still worthy of love, no matter what. Her little nudges were telling me, 'I love you Kylie and always will, don't worry.' As I quickly realised this as her gift to me, tears of regret flowed from my eyes and love from my heart and soul. I realised I had taken it out on her by been impatient with her and ignoring her trying to comfort me. She was trying to communicate to me that she loved me and was there for me and that she understood how I felt.

From that day onwards I chose to serve her forever and since making that decision I have felt totally liberated and at peace. The love of God now works through me all the time and connects to horses; we become one with our creator. We were ever so grateful to have found each other.

Once we become aware of our inner-self and start to observe how we could be contributing to the current problems we are experiencing with our horses, we start to see that training our horse from demand and controlling ways are not going to give us positive experiences with our horses. They respond positively to a kind loving approach, with clear boundaries set for them. It is us that have to learn this from them. I realised every time I saw beauty by looking at my horse; I was in fact seeing my own beauty. The more I focused on seeing her beauty, the more I saw my inner beauty. I started to see her movement flow naturally with such grace and elegance. She knew she was a sight and loved to show off. I started to say to her, 'beautiful girl, show me what you've got' and she did.' She excelled and I praised her more and more, telling her how clever she was.

I encouraged her to express her beauty that God had gifted her with and I embraced my own. By me embracing my own inner beauty, I was allowing her to do the same. She was really only mirroring back to me, how I felt myself.

I started to really become excited about my life and saw our relationship as a very spiritual one. It was all about me growing to find more love within myself, not about her at all.

I started to be grateful for her offering me this opportunity to see through her what I needed to work on within myself. I knew by doing this for myself and her, we would have a healthy wonderful life together.

Then everything else in my life seemed to fall into place, flow and become balanced. Doors opened for me and my heart began to sing in every area of my life.

It doesn't matter what you are training your horse, all you need to remember is to come from love, feel it, become it, express it and be it. It is your divine right as a spiritual being. Always hold the vision of the end goal you want to see yourself and your horse doing. Your horse will feel your love and see your vision, never let this vision go, hold onto it and don't let anything bump you off your course, for you will achieve it my dear ones. Enjoy the journey; for it is a magnificent one with these amazing, delightful equine companions I call 'divine beings' of grace.

Training your horse spiritually allows your horse to stay relaxed in its work

Dear Jess
May I sit on your back
May I become one with your spirit
May the spirit flow through us
While we ride and dance together
in peace and harmony
always
Thank you for allowing me to share this wonderful
experience
with you
You are a beautiful girl
by
Kylie Maree Dearden

Chapter 10:

Riding Your Horse Spiritually

I have always been in awe that humans have been able to share a special bond with such a strong and powerful animal as the horse. Being able to ride them, even being able to get close enough to touch them has always been a special gift to me. I believe it's a gift from God. As I spent time with my horse I began to notice at times when I was annoyed at myself for not knowing how to ride a movement well that I was learning to ride on her, that she was so understanding and patient with me. I realised it was me being too hard on myself. I was the one who had to let it go and to focus on becoming the best rider I could be, by staying positive within myself through growth and change with her. I started to see I would receive much more with her by maintaining this outlook towards myself and her. I soon realised that I loved her so much and was so grateful to her for allowing me to ride her and share this special bond that I just wanted to be the best rider I could be for her. So that she would be comfortable at all times while I was riding her. This is when I decided to complete a horse course and have riding lessons with several different instructors.

I was interested in dressage most of all as this seemed to be the most natural movements for the horse to perform; they just looked so graceful and elegant. Horses did these movements naturally as a foal, with such grace and ease. To me they were dancing and expressing themselves. I was excited to think of being able to share this graceful experience with my horse and what a gift it would be for me. I knew I would be a more enlightened being by expressing my divinity and love through riding and connecting with her what I felt in my heart and soul. I liked the idea of being able to share this experience with my horse, but only if the horse wanted to and never was I willing to force my horse into sharing this experience with me. As I grew with my horse and trained her through the different levels of dressage, I would always thank her throughout these training sessions. As I did this I could see her wanting to give more and more, she was really enjoying this time we spent together. She just loves rewards of 'good girl Jess, you are such a clever and talented girl.' What can I say, I just love to love her and I could see by me loving and appreciating her I was also loving and approving of myself and our confidence grew stronger and stronger every day. Instructors used to say to me, stop loving her so much, however I couldn't help myself, it was the spirit within me that was the driving force within as I was riding her. People should never be frightened in giving their horse love. As you ride your horse with love they will relax and learn a lot faster than if you demand and not appreciate your horse. Calm correction is needed when the horse is confused or unsure of what you are wanting.

When your horse receives love from you it relaxes, love motivates your horse to want to try harder and please you. Love is the answer if you wish to achieve harmony with them. I guarantee it! It's always worked for me and I know it always will. Patience is another requirement in finding harmony with your horse but then again, isn't patience love too?

As I realised that love was the answer to finding harmony with my horse, I couldn't wait to see her each day, to see what she had to teach me that day about myself. To be able to smell her, touch her and connect with her was a gift that I knew and embraced. When I was with her nothing else mattered. I developed my riding skills more and became in touch with my intuition through yoga and mediation. As I began to combine the two, my riding experience with her became much better. By being connected to my soul now, I was riding my horse spiritually and what a huge difference it made. I moved around from instructor to instructor until I found one I felt comfortable with. I learnt what I needed to know until I was ready to go out on my own. I brought videos, books and later connected more to my inner spirit and wisdom which guided me to finding harmony with my horse. I now felt ready after having nine years of instruction.

I was coming from my soul's love towards my horse and had the knowledge and understanding to take her further in her training to the higher levels of dressage. Riding Jess became such a rewarding experience for both of us. We would just grow more and more. It was wonderful to watch her develop and grow. I always do stretches to warm up my body as I first get on her to ride, followed by prayers and positive affirmations. I also thank Jess for allowing me to ride her and ask for her permission and willingness. Always thanking God, the universal energy, for looking after us both and helping us come together to be one with our creator in peace and harmony.

I always say to Jess at the beginning, I choose to love you not hurt you during this time we spend together. I start to feel the beautiful blissful energy of the Universe flow through me and feel very relaxed. I watch her reaction to my aids at all times and if she shows me signs of feeling uncomfortable or confused I listen to her and look at how I might have contributed to this via a negative thought or tension in my body during a movement that I have found difficult. At these times I have found practicing a yoga pose by taking a deep breath and rolling my shoulders back during the movement helpful this allows my body to stay relaxed. I am also able to ride with a clear focused mind and very aware of my inner self and body due to lots of spiritual development and meditation classes over many years. I cannot stress enough if we are to find harmony with our horses and most important ourselves, practicing daily yoga and meditation is essential. I love it and I'm sure you will too. It's very relaxing and worth it, it can be done at the basic to advanced levels and in 15 minute sessions.

While you're riding and interacting with horses you really need to tell the ego to take a back seat. It only gets in the way and creates negative experiences between you and your horse. Ask yourself what you are trying to prove to yourself, in God's eyes and in your horse's eyes you are already perfect, whole and complete. So let go of any false idea that you'll be more loved and approved of if you win a ribbon. At the end of the day who are you competing with or against, yourself? We are all unique and special in our own way and so is our horse. I'm not against competing; I did it myself for years. I felt it was what I wanted to do at that time. I do appreciate what I learnt from it. You always learn something from everything you do. I allowed my instructors at the time to convince me that I should be competing as I had the horse to do it with, that most people would give anything to have. Notice how I said, 'I allowed myself to be convinced', that's because we always have a choice to go with what feels right for us at the time. This is so important to remember – if it doesn't feel right, don't do it. There is something else for you coming your way more to your liking. All I'm saying is please don't let winning a competition become more important than loving and bonding with your horse and doing what's right for both of your health and well being. Never let the ego take first place. If you do you will be denying yourself and your horse a special experience that I call – freedom!

Riding your horse spiritually – Jess and I riding in a dressage competition

Dear one
As I connect
and communicate
With you
I send you healing
and comfort
Love & peace
by
Kylie Maree Dearden

Chapter 11:

Communicating with Horses

Ever since I was a little girl I understood horse's emotions and like any young girl who was growing and developing, I was unaware that this was a gift. I was unaware not all of us could understand horses' body language. I thought everyone knew what they were saying and how they felt. It wasn't until I started to study spirituality and meditation that I became aware that I had been reading horse's body language all along and knew what they were trying to tell me. I began to understand that in their presence my mind became still and I would feel this inner peace and harmony being around them. This is when I was able to tune into their (energy) and became aware. I started to really notice this when I would spend time with my horse, grooming her and talking to her. She would touch me with her nose in response to what I was saying. For a long time I used to answer her all the time, knowing exactly what she was saying. I took this as normal, until I realised no one else did it. I treated a horse thoroughbred mare, which was 10-years-old, that had been on the race track till five- years-old and now my client was going to event with her.

I was to give a healing treatment to this mare as she was showing signs of nervousness. She had been out of work for three months when my client had taken her on board. As I first approached the horse I knew something was wrong. I then noticed how lost she was and confused at what was going on. She didn't know what was expected of her from this new owner or even why she was leased out. She was looking so much to bond and feel secure. This mare told me with her body communication that she wanted to find an owner who had faith in her and who she could trust. The client was excited to tell me she had jumped her over one metre high already. I was happy for her but could see she was clearly focused on status quo rather than bonding and loving the horse. My client continued to tell me that she felt a little unsafe with the mare as she went over the jump; she lifted her head and nearly hit my client in the face. The mare was frightened and was trying to get my client's attention. 'I'm frightened please don't make me jump this height yet. I don't feel confident enough yet, in you or myself,' the horse was telling her. Before I realised I had a gift to be able to understand my horse's feelings and emotions, I would push my horse away when she tried to talk and communicate with me. I was in a hurry most of the time and when she would nudge me, I didn't see then that she was trying to connect and communicate with me. I would say 'no, not now, I don't have time, to bond with you, I've got to go.' I soon realised like anyone who wants attention and to be noticed, the more I ignored her, the worse she got. I started to realise she was just like a child, showing me with her body language of her disapproval. She would stomp her front leg, then back, then shake her head and look at me, throwing a little tantrum.

Intuitively, I knew what she was saying to me. I read her body language which said, 'I don't understand why you can't touch and connect with me; all I want to do is love you and show you how much.' At that moment I read her communication,

I looked at her in the eye and she had this look in her eye like she was hurting emotionally and felt rejected. I thought how open she is to being loved by me; I stopped in my tracks as any person would with this awareness as I knew what she was trying to communicate to me. I embraced her around the neck; she showed me how much she loved being with me. I can't tell you enough in words how special that moment was for both of us. It was like we became one with God – the Universe. It was at this moment that our relationship had a complete turn around. I told my client 'if you wish your horse to jump without lifting her head and feeling frightened you're going to need to show your horse that your need to love and bond with her is more important than her making that jump.' 'You are going to need to practice her at basic jumps until she gets more confident before expecting her to jump this height.

You are also going to need to spend time bonding with her and build a relationship to develop trust. Once she feels love and trusts you she will gain confidence and you will jump mountains, believe you me. Love always has to be the basis for anything to flourish and perform at its best. For me it's more important that my horse is relaxed and happy in the time we spend together.

Before I started communicating with horses, I had been meditating daily for many years and taking spiritual development classes before I had these experiences on a deep level with my horse and other horses. I also practiced yoga often and was so grateful to have the ability to be able to understand horse's feelings and emotions.

What a rewarding relationship we had through me being able to do this. Jess would show me how she loves to smell me and always sniffs my hair and nuzzles me on my neck for minutes at a time and we embraced the love we have for each other. When she wants to play she gives me a nudge on my arm with her nose and I either tickle her on the nose with my fingers or let her lick my hand or sometimes I grab her head with both my hands and hug her. She loves to play like this and as I don't always have lots of time to spare, I just have a quick play with her and then continue grooming her. She then decides to show me how clever she is by undoing the quick release knot I have tied her up to, which allows her to reach her carrots in my tack box. Most of the time she succeeds but I trick her now as I tie the knot in a way it makes it difficult for her to undo. The only thing is it's no longer a quick release knot so most of the time I just end up playing with her. She's not silly, is she now? I tell her she is a cheeky girl, who I dearly love and wouldn't change for the world. She is so smart, never underestimate a horse's intelligence, the more contact we have with them the more they learn and the smarter they become. It's amazing what they show you as time goes on. The more you love them, the happier they are and the more they express their personalities in this playful way. It's more important we take time to play with horses that are in separate yards as they sometimes can't touch and connect with other horses. While I know another horse can't give her the same relationship that we share, horses still give each-other company and protection that can help prevent behaviour patterns from developing.

My horse shows me she loves the human contact.

Part of this has to do with the healing abilities I have developed (which I will discuss in another chapter). Jess loves to connect with me on a spiritual level and enjoys it when I ride her. As long as I'm coming from love and not ego when I am riding her, she loves it. She also enjoys the universal healing energy that flows through us when we ride. I ask to be connected to this energy as I begin to ride her. I do stretches as I warm her up in walk and say prayers. I find this helps me stay relaxed and focused while I ride her and offers Jess healing energy. I ask God I only wish to come from love as I interact with my horse at all times and that she is comfortable at all times while I am riding her. I always thank her and the Universe for allowing us to share this special bond.

If we take the time to listen to and observe our horse's body language and learn to feel and understand our horses' emotions, we will eliminate most behavioural problems we face with horses that arise. If we don't take the time to listen and observe our horses, then be prepared for a fight plus unnecessary conflict and disharmony between you and your horse. This leads to frustration and sometimes injury and hurt towards horse and rider. As we all know when we are frightened or angry like our horses this can lead to danger to them and us. It's also quite possible the horse may be hurting physically somewhere and this is usually able to be proven by the vet or horse chiropractor.

Communicating with Jess

Dearest one
I know you
are
hurting
I'm sorry
for your
pain
God wants
you to know
you are
dearly loved
by
Kylie Maree Dearden

Chapter 12:

Why Horses Develop Behavioural Problems

Horses aren't naturally born with behavioural problems, just like people aren't. It is the way horses have been treated and handled that depends on whether the horse develops behavioural problems or not. When a horse is hard to handle, it is trying to tell us something. It is up to us to listen to them and observe their body language and body behaviour, as they have most likely suffered emotional, mental, physical or spiritual pain in the past.

The horse's behavioural problem is not going to go away by us trying to overpower them with more demands and expectations. If we stop and listen, then observe the horse will straight away see you are not just there to take from them but also to give. Taking the time to try and understand their pain means a lot to them. Their pain could possibly be yours or a hurtful experience from the past they are still suffering from. If you wish to find harmony with your horse and to understand your horse's emotions, start looking at your own. The horse may be offering you a chance to heal your own emotional pain or may just have come into your life to help you grow.

By looking at your own emotions and inner self, you are able to release any hurtful feelings that you may be holding onto from the past, which needs to be released. Horses take on all of our emotions and it is only by healing ourselves by thinking loving, kind thoughts towards ourselves and our horses that we will find peace with them and ourselves. I also recommend healing treatments to be given to the horse and yourself from time to time as this helps release a build-up of negative toxins within the aura field and body (I will discuss this further in my chapter on healing horses).

If we are really honest with ourselves and look at the way we treat our horses, we will soon see if we are coming from love, fear or anger and resentment while interacting with them. God did not intend horses to suffer. It is our own beliefs that cause us such pain and suffering and that hold us back from enjoying a loving bond and relationship with our horses. Once we release our negative thoughts and replace them with positive loving thoughts, we will notice a big difference in our horse's reaction towards us. Thoughts are energy, which travel and connect to our horses. They affect our horses and everyone around us. It's so important we keep them pure. It's time to start looking at how we train and handle our horses. We are not getting positive results out of horses that have been trained and handled in a manner where they are forced into submission, by someone in an egotistical state of mind, who is trying to misuse their power over the horse so it submits through fear. This is not going to bring harmony between you and your horse or create trust and respect.

The horse will never trust or relax or develop to its fullest potential if they are trained in this manner. Most of all they will not lead a life of inner peace and well being. This is why I believe I see so many frightened, angry and fed up horses everywhere I go. It saddens me to see and feel their pain.

God gave us a gift to be able to share this special bond and relationship with these amazing animals. Let's not take advantage of God's will. Whenever we come from anger, demand or power to dominate our horses we go against God's wishes and will. God gave us these beautiful horses to heal us and the planet and to share a special bond with them of love and friendship. When the horse knows you come from love instead of ego towards them, they will respect and trust you, they will want to please you once you have explained in a kind but firm way the boundaries and what you wish to experience and share with them. The horse will respect and see you as its leader and guide. It will feel comfortable knowing that it will be respected and loved when it is spending time with you. It knows you have its best interests at heart and it will honour and serve you for this as you honour and serve them.

Just imagine if horses could choose their owners, ask yourself, would your horse choose you? Do you think of its well being and happiness as much as your own and sometimes before your own, if you have to?

I often think my horse is due for a massage or healing treatment now and because she can't just go off and book herself in for one like I can, I need to do this for her. At these times I put her first. My horse amazes me with the love she gives to me. I'm sure there are times she is a little tired but she still keeps going for me, without letting me know. I make sure I monitor her every step of the way and if I feel she needs a rest, I let go of needing to achieve anything that day and put her well being first – always! It's always best, I find, to leave her training to another day when she is more refreshed. I let go the ego needing to achieve anything today. I go with the flow of the Universe – God the spirit within that knows you are perfect, whole and complete right here and right now. At times I am hard on myself when learning a new movement on her and I know she picks this up in my body language, energy and thoughts. I've noticed she can get a little anxious when I'm hard on myself and I need to reassure her and stay relaxed for her, for example if I'm not happy with a transition in collected trot, I simply ask her for working trot, get her relaxed and forward, then try asking for the collected trot transition again, then reward her as I achieve the desired response from her I am looking for. Sometimes she thinks I am disappointed with her when I do this. I just talk to her with my voice and tell her 'it's alright you didn't do anything wrong, I just need to get it right for you.' Most of the time it's me that needs to understand the right aids she needs from me, to perform the movement the best she can. Sometimes I even halt her and ask her to let it go and tell her she is my beautiful girl who I dearly love and we are getting better and better every day.

She then feels reassured and relaxes. I find my training with her gets ahead a lot quicker and she is getting what she needs to enjoy this experience with me. I say to her, "I am so grateful to you for allowing me to share this very special bond with you, thank you." It makes my heart sing to be with her and to love her. She amazes me in her ability to figure it all out for me. By loving her, believing and encouraging her, she just shines more and more everyday. I'm always telling her how talented she is. Her ability to grasp new movements in a flash blows me away. I often tell her how proud of her I am and when I look into her eyes, she knows and responds with the most gentle nudge on my arm followed by a kiss with her muzzle on my neck. She feels my love for her and I was grateful and surprised to experience all horses responded to me this way. I believe it's because they all feel the energy and love I have for them. It's eternal; it can never die because it's the spirit within me that salutes the spirit in them. All horses know I honour, respect and serve them. I believe it's because of this I gain the horses trust and respect.

Dearest one
May I touch you
I offer to heal you
not hurt you
I offer to love you
not harm you
Bless you
Dear one
By
Kylie Maree Dearden

Chapter 13:

Healing Horses

Never in my wildest dreams did I ever imagine I would get a chance to repay my horse for all the help she gave me through the difficult times I had experienced in my life. Loving her and appreciating her never seemed to be enough. As I developed my spiritual gifts as a healer and experienced this blissful loving energy flowing through my body while I was performing healing treatments on horses, I was amazed to be experiencing this. I wanted to know how and why I was gifted to be experiencing this. So then I was led to two books that would explain what I was experiencing and why – *The Power of Intention* – by Dr Wayne W. Dyer and *Power Vs Force* (an anatomy of consciousness) by David R. Hawkins M.D, PhD. In these extraordinary books I became aware that during my healing treatments, my consciousness level was vibrating at an energy level of 600: peace and rise higher at times to (enlightenment) – this energy field is associated with the experience designated by such terms as transcendence, self-realization and God-consciousness. This awesome revelation takes place non-rationally so that there is an infinite silence in the mind, which has stopped conceptualizing. Everything is connected to everything else by a presence whose power is infinite. As I would start to feel this divine energy flow through me I received words of grace and divinity towards my horse.

This would explain to me why my horse would start to sigh several times and drop her head as she entered my aura field. I always feel this extreme heat in the palm of my hands and feet. As I move my hands and touch things I feel tingling in the palms of my hands. I learnt that I was gifted to reach this high state of grace and that at these times I was accessing the higher energy field vibrations of the universe, which enabled me to heal.

I was so grateful to be experiencing this. The best part of this awareness, I discovered, was I felt I was able to give back to my horse all that she had given to me and more. Any pain or discomfort she may have felt during my learning process to become a better rider and owner, I was now able to offer her healing back. I was now giving her back what she had given to me. I thought what a miracle, a true blessing! After I completed my Reiki 2 course in 2004, in tradition of the Usui method of natural healing, I had a strong desire to want to heal horses. I did not know at that stage anyone else who performed healing treatments on horses, so I let it be and carried on with my life. After a few months had gone by, I was led to a book called *Healing for Horses* by Margrit Coates who was based in the UK and performed healing treatments on horses. I believe my spirit guided me to this book, this is how it happened. One day as I was waiting for my horse's rug to be repaired, I decided to browse around the shop. I never noticed this horse store to have a book stand before, but being a lover of horse books, I decided to browse over the books and the book *Healing for Horses* jumped out at me. As I picked it up I felt this blissful energy of grace emanate through my entire body, which confirmed to me this book was meant for me. As I read it, the blissful energy was flowing through me the whole time and reading the book I was to learn that I had been intuitively healing my horse the whole time.

I had the same gift as Margrit Coates did and was grateful to the Universe for leading me to this valuable information and realization. As I began to learn about the horse's chakra (energy) centres and also more about how the healing energy in the Universe works, I began to study energy more and learnt the word "spirit" means vital animating essence of a person or animal, so the term spiritual healing means – universal healing of that vital essence within the body. Anyone has the ability to heal who chooses to be a healing person rather than a hurting person. There is no hierarchy to follow; it is your own personal relationship with the healing power that determines how much the horse will benefit from the healing. The horse will benefit the most by a person who is a pure clear channel for the healing energy of the Universe. What I mean by this is one who can clear and quiet their mind and connect to their highest self where the energy and words of love and wisdom are channelled to the horse going to that part of the horse's body where the healing is needed most. The actual source of the problem may lie deep in the horse and could have been triggered off a long time ago, often many years before the current condition appeared. By strengthening the horse's body with healing and by achieving homeostasis, it is hoped that the horse will respond and begin to repair or stabilize from within. Healing can work emotionally, mentally, physically or spiritually during a treatment. Energy is transferred via the healer to the animal and travels down the lines of energy in the horse's body called (meridians). When we are creators of beneficial and positive energy, it allows us to release destructive energy into the Universe. The healers use physical energy (via their hands), mental energy (through their minds) and emotional energy (through feelings of love) to treat the horse holistically).

The mind is open, focused with intent peaceful thoughts attuned to the creative source and harmonizes with the infinite intelligence. The heart is open, loving, empathetic, compassionate and giving and the hands are a link that channels healing energy (healing touch). In other words, hands-on healing aims to help on all levels by restoring balance of homeostasis.

As I studied and practiced meditation for years I was aware of the seven chakra centres within the human body. Chakra's are whirlpools of energy found in various parts of the body and relate to physical, emotional and mental health. Chakra's are linked one to the other and have a negative and positive polarity. As we align our chakra centres through meditation, these energy centres become balanced and we are then able to access the higher positive energies of the Universe which flow through our body and raise our energy levels to a higher frequency. Energy from the chakra's can be felt by the hands and sensitive individuals can also see colours emit from them. This positive energy is channelled through the healer's body and hands. This universal healing energy runs along pathways within the horse's body, known as meridians. The vital energy force flows along these meridians. These meridians emit light and can be seen using infra-red photography. An electromagnetic field surrounds and penetrates the physical body and influences what happens on the physical level. These fields can be photographed and filmed. Study of electromagnetic qualities has shown they are associated with channels and energy points – chakra throughout the body. Similarly, an energy field is radiated outwards from the Earth and is called the geomagnetic field.

The healer is the channel for the spiritual force of the universal healing energy. This source provides the electromagnetic fingerprint, or blueprint, to match what is missing in the horse. This energy is channelled to the horse at its chakra centres at the deepest levels by the healer and can work physically, mentally, emotionally or spiritually. Brain wave patterns of the healer pulse in unison with the Earth's magnetic field, known as the Schumann Resonance. Research has shown that the wave patterns of the healer and receiver synchronize in the alpha state, characteristic of meditation and deep relaxation.

As I became aware that this was one of my gifts, I was a healer; I then began to understand why I had always felt so connected to horses. There was a divine reason why we had been brought together and I started to discover a life purpose which I had to fulfil. So much so it made my heart sing to bring them peace of any kind by channelling through the universal healing energy. To see the peace in their faces and to leave them in a deep relaxed state was so rewarding for me. What can I say, I love to love them. This is what I enjoy most and what I am here to do. I feel so privileged to be able to get close to these beautiful animals. I started to realise the Great Spirit was using me as a tool to thank them for all the love and healing they bring to the planet. As the universal healing energy channelled through me during a healing treatment, I would receive inspirational words from spirit, "hello dear one, please accept this love as a gift for all you have given to humanity and the world. You are a beautiful and beloved spirit of God, who is dearly loved.

"I ask that all negative energy you have received from the past be released and that the light of God and the angels protects you for your highest good God bless you dear one." The horse sighs several times and usually drops its head to the ground.

After the healing treatment, the horse often leans over to nuzzle me with its nose and says "Thank you".

I then say "You are welcome dear one, by you accepting spirit's love that channels through me, you give me a great gift."

My spiritual experiences while performing healing treatments on horses

The Universe led me to horses that needed healing. As I performed healing treatments, I had many experiences, emotionally, mentally and physically. As I used extra sensory during my healing treatments by tuning into the horses energy field, I began to feel physical tension within the horse's body through my body. I felt where the blockages and damages were within the horse's physical body. I experienced each horse had blockages in different places and I realised where these blockages were and how severe they were depended on the horse's past experiences and events. The common areas where I feel physical tension in my body while I tuned into the horse's energy field are mainly in the head area, back and hind quarters. I usually experience a vibrating within my arms and hands on the chakra's centres that are most imbalanced. The healing universal energy life force channels through stronger at these energy points.

As the universal healing energy is rebalancing the horse's mental, emotional and physical state, I usually feel the most imbalance in the solar plexus centres (horses' emotions) and root chakra centres (physical problems). On an emotional level as I channel through the universal healing energy, I often become overwhelmed all of a sudden with emotions and begin to cry expressing and releasing the horse's hurt feelings.

I always feel a great sense of relief in my body once I have released the horse's emotions and I have a feeling of inner peace and calmness within. On a mental level as I channel through the universal healing energy and tune into the horse's feelings and emotions, I received the feeling that the horses were frightened, confused and felt unsafe and unloved.

I reassure them they are dearly loved and that we are open to growing and understanding them more. I apologise for any pain they have suffered and ask them for their forgiveness. I advise them we are just doing the best we can with the knowledge and understanding that we have at this time in our lives. I thank them for their patience and understanding.

As I performed my first healing treatment on my horse, she became very agitated as the healing energy began activating and releasing the negative energy from her body that she had been carrying. She was nudging me with her nose quite forcefully, showing me how she felt the disturbed energy leaving her body. I asked her to please release it as she would feel much better and more at peace.

I communicated to her that it was safe for her to relax and release anything in her body that was not serving her any good and that I would protect her. All of a sudden I began to feel emotional and burst out crying, tears streamed down my face as I released her hurt feelings. She communicated and showed me with her body language that she had been confused at times during her training and felt unsure of what was expected of her and why. I felt all she wanted was to feel loved and secure. She had lost trust in people when I met her and had built up walls to protect herself from further pain. I apologised for this happening to her. I promised her I would love and take care of her. She could feel safe with me. I said to her 'sweetie I will never take advantage of your kindness and I will never leave you.' She dropped her head to the ground and gave a big sigh of relief. I held her in my arms for some time and prayed.

Giving love a healing treatment

Giving Jess a healing treatment

Dearest God
Forgive me please
for not knowing
how hurt my horse was
I see clearly now
what I am to do
May I always be an
expression of your love
I am ever so grateful
by
Kylie Maree Dearden

Chapter 14:

Positive Affirmations I Say to My Horse

I always listen to my horse's
Feelings and messages and respond
to them with patience and love

I am always open to my horse's
messages on how I can learn to
love her more
I am willing to grow

I focus on being positive at all
times with my thoughts and body
language while connecting with
my horse today

It makes my heart sing to
love and connect with my
horse's spirit today

I express my gratitude and
appreciation to my horse for
allowing me to bond and ride
with her

I never take advantage of my
horse's kindness and patience
I thank her at every moment
I have faith in myself and
my horse, we grow
together more & more
every day

My horse and I express the
greatness that we are
today and every day

My horse and I are divine
Magnificent expression of
life and we honour the divinity
within us

I say to my horse, I
salute the divinity within you,
I honour you, I serve you,
for your unconditional
Love

My horse and I move from success
to success, joy to joy and abundance
to abundance
We are one with the power
that created us

My horse and I move into our
divineness, we express
the greatness that we are

My horse and I express our natural talents and
abilities we excel at everything we do

My horse and I deserve the best and
we accept the best now

I practice staying calm and
connected to the spirit
within at all times while
I ride my horse today

My horse and I are a beautiful
expression of life

I create a peaceful, loving,
environment for my horse
to feel safe in

As I ride my beautiful horse today
love is all around me
It flows through me
every step of the way

My horse and I come together
in peace and harmony today and
everyday, we are dearly
loved by the Universe

This day my horse and I choose
to see the good in all no matter what
we show love, compassion and understanding
to all we come in contact with

My horse and I express happiness and
joy from our entire being today and
everyday

I say to my horse,
"Let's dance
let's celebrate life"
My horse and I love life

My horse and I flow with the
spirit of life

we ride together in
peace and harmony

My horse and I embrace life
with joy and gratitude

My horse and I ride this
day with grace and ease

As I ride my horse today
I think thoughts of love
beauty, peace and harmony

Today my horse and I express
our soul's deepest love
for each other

This day I offer my horse compassion
love and understanding as we
spend time together

My horse and I always ride
together relaxed and
at ease

My horse and I give great
thanks to spirit for
guiding and protecting us
today and every day

My horse and I are always safe
in the Universe as we
spend time together

Affirmations are part of the process to 'finding

harmony with your horse'. They will help you stay focused with a loving mindset to create positive experiences with your horse.

These affirmations I wrote came to me during my meditation sessions. I enjoy using them often, as they give me a heightened experience with my horse as I spend time with her. I hope you enjoy them too!

Happy horsing!

Chapter 15:

Horses Heal Us

As I awoke on the morning of August 30th 2004, I received words from spirit, "inner reflection, your horse mirrors your inner self." If we wish find peace and harmony with our horses, we must first find it within ourselves.

Horses offer us a wonderful opportunity to heal ourselves from past emotional pain we have suffered, by offering to love us unconditionally through our healing process.

As horses are able to offer us this priceless gift and healing opportunity, we owe it to them to offer them love back they give so much to us. All they want is to be noticed, loved and appreciated.

Horses know us inside and out, they hear and feel our thoughts and they are linked to us spiritually. This is why it is so important to be aware of our thoughts while we are interacting with these amazing animals. For thoughts are energy, feelings in motion, moving through our body to our horse. If we have a negative thought such as anger, fear, guilt or resentment, our horse will feel this and mirror it back to us. Hence, if we have a positive thought of love for example, we will create a positive experience with our horse.

Unfortunately, horses take on the owner's emotions like most animals do. They rely on us so much to think positive for them. By thinking positive for them, we are in turn doing the right thing for ourselves.

By the horse mirroring our negative thoughts back to us via their body language, they offer us an opportunity to heal. Heal from our pain of not feeling loved, approved of etc. If we would only listen to them and observe them, we would see there is a message in every response we receive from them.

This is why it is best not to interact with our horses if we are tired, angry or upset for the horse will respond towards us these negative feelings and emotions and become difficult to handle. Not only will we be causing our horse to feel our pain, we will in return be feeling our pain back via our horse's reactions and responses.

As horses offer us this opportunity to heal ourselves from past pain and hurt and to share a very special bond with them, it is crucial that we never take advantage of their kindness and their ability to love us unconditionally. It is our responsibility to never abuse our horse's kindness of nature and the amount of love they give us.

They allow us to share this beautiful relationship with them. It is against all spiritual law of God's will to ever take anger out on these wonderful animals. They trust us, they rely on us to love them, care for them and guide them to safety and a life filled with peace and harmony.

Thanking Jess for the joy, peace and love she has brought into my life